The Story of the Cowboys

US History Books
Children's American History

In this book, we're going to cover the important role that cowboys played during the Western expansion of the United States. So, let's get right to it!

WHAT IS A
COWBOY?

The word "cowboy" first appeared in the English vocabulary by 1725. It was a translation from the word "vaquero," which meant a man who managed herds of cattle while he was riding a horse.

Another word for cowboy is the word "buckaroo" and it's also an English version of the word "vaquero."

Though the "cowboy" is considered to be American, the roots of the tradition began in Spain, eventually spreading to Mexico and the Southwest of the US.

Many ranch owners in Mexico had Spanish ancestors, but the vaqueros were frequently Native Americans who had been trained to care for herds belonging to the Spanish missions.

As the Western expansion of the United States continued, English-speaking settlers brought English traditions and these mixed with the existing Spanish culture and language.

Before 1848, merchants from England traveled to California by ship. There they encountered the ranch owners, called hacendados, and the vaqueros. These ranchers were trading hides from their cattle for manufactured goods.

Along the region that was eventually called the Santa Fe trail,
traders from the US became familiar with the life and traditions
of the vaqueros.

Eventually, these traditions produced the iconic American cowboy that we know today.

In Texas, English-speaking settlers began to arrive around 1821. There were wild horses and lots of free-roaming cattle that had been left by the Mexicans when they were ordered to leave the lands between the Nueces and the Rio Grande.

The Texians, citizens of Texas when it was still governed by Mexico, raided these wild creatures for their use. Texas became independent from Mexico in 1836.

After the Mexican-American War from 1846-1848, English-speaking settlers came to California as well. In the war, Mexico lost about one-third of its land including almost all of California, New Mexico, Utah, Nevada, and Arizona.

This huge expansion of ranching land, and the mixing of the vaquero lifestyle from Mexico to the West and Southwest of the rapidly growing US, is what led to the rise of the American cowboy.

Once the railroads arrived, there was an increased demand for beef. The cattle drives began at the ranches where the cattle were raised and ended hundreds of miles away at the nearest railheads.

In the 1880s, after the Civil War, the cattle industry expanded even further into the northwest where there were large regions of open grassland.

Cowboys adapted their gear to the cooler temperatures and the cultures of both Californian and Texan cowboys intermingled as the best traditions of each blended together.

Over a period of time, American cowboys developed a unique culture of their own. It was a blend of independent frontier values with a dose of Old-World Victorian values. It even had some components of medieval knights and chivalry.

The work cowboys did was very dangerous and they were often isolated for long periods of time.

Cowboys became rugged, independent individuals who prided themselves on honesty. The songs and poetry of the times expressed this true Western self-sufficient spirit.

WILD WEST
SHOWS

Wild West shows were traveling performances that showcased American cowboys. The first Wild West show was Buffalo Bill's, first performed in 1883.

These shows were very popular in both the United States and Europe. Of course, just like any form of entertainment, the Wild West shows were not a true depiction of the life of cowboys in the West.

They showed a romanticized view of the Western lifestyle, which continued into television and movies decades later.

Because there were a lot of skills needed to become a cowboy, a young man usually started to learn the trade around the age of 12 or 13. As soon as he had enough skill to be hired he was earning wages.

If he wasn't injured during the dangerous cattle drives, he might work with cattle or horses for the rest of his life.

There were girls and women who tackled difficult ranching tasks as well but the "cowgirl" didn't become recognized until the end of the 19th century, when cowgirls performed in Wild West Shows and rodeos.

Cowboys played a critical role in the expansion of the West.

Ranching was a huge industry and the cowboys handled all the work needed to keep the ranch running efficiently. They herded the wayward cattle, fixed fences and repaired buildings as well as groomed and fed the horses.

One of the most important roles the cowboy played was when driving the cattle to market. By driving here, we don't mean that the cowboys put the cattle in trucks!

These cattle "drives" were just herds of cattle that had to walk from where they were on the ranch to their final destination. A lot of the first cattle drives went from Texas all the way to the Kansas railroads. The cattle drive was tough work and very dangerous.

Cowboys would get up at the crack of dawn to guide the herd to the next location before nightfall. They worked on horseback with about a dozen men for every 3,000 head of cattle.

Senior cowboys were typically at the front of the huge herd. The junior cowboys were "left in the dust" at the end of the herd.

In addition to the dozen or so cowboys that were in charge of the drive, there was usually a trail boss as well as a cook who made the food and a wrangler. As a junior cowboy, the wrangler's job was to keep track of the extra horses.

THE ROUNDUP

During the year, cattle roamed freely on the open range. In order for ranchers to determine which cattle were theirs, they burned a symbol into the animal's hide that was their special brand.

This brand would generally have the initials associated with the owner of the ranch. In the early spring and also in the fall, the cowboys would "roundup" the cattle and bring them in.

HORSES AND
SADDLES

The most prized possessions belonging to a cowboy were his horse and his saddle. Next to his trusty horse, a custom-made saddle was the most valuable item he owned.

Horses were so vital that if it was proven that you had stolen a horse, you would be hanged to death.

HOW DO COWBOYS DRESS?

Western wear grew out of the needs of the harsh environments where cowboys worked. Each piece of clothing had a very specific function.

The bandanna is a neckerchief that helped the cowboy wipe sweat from his brow and protected his face from dust.

Chaps are leggings attached to a belt. Cowboys wore these to protect their legs when riding through brush or when herding livestock.

Boots had high tops to shield the lower legs and their pointed toes made it easy for the cowboy to get his feet into the stirrups.

The pointed toes also made it easier for the cowboy to detach his feet from the stirrups if he fell off his horse. The tall heels of the boots were designed to keep his feet from slipping through the stirrups.

Cowboy hats had high crowns and wide brims to protect them from the blazing sun and overhanging tree limbs.

There were many styles of cowboy hats designed by famous hat manufacturer, John Batterson Stetson. They were made especially for the harsh climate of the West.

To protect their hands, cowboys wore gloves made of leather or deerskin. This made it possible for them to work with barbed wire and scratchy native brush.

Cowboys made jeans popular as well. These tight-fitting trousers made of denim were made to shield their legs from getting caught on native brush or equipment. They also had smooth inside seams to protect their legs from blistering while on horseback.

TOOLS OF
THE TRADE

In addition to a good rifle and pistol for protection, cowboys carried pocket knives for cutting.

They also carried ropes called lariats from the Spanish words "la riata" meaning "the rope." These stiff ropes made from rawhide were made with a small loop called a "hondo."

When the rope was pushed through the hondo, it created a loop that tightened down quickly around the neck of an animal. This made it possible for the cowboy to throw the rope at a distance and then lasso a running animal to capture it.

The heels of a cowboy's boots had metal devices called spurs. They had a metal shank with a serrated wheel. These spurs gave the cowboy a way to "spur on" his horse to move faster as he rounded up the herd.

In the old West, cowboys worked very hard but they only made about $25 a month, which is about $680 in today's dollars.

Awesome! Now you know more how influential cowboys were in history of the American West. You can find more American History books from Baby Professor by searching the website of your favorite book retailer.

Visit
BABY PROFESSOR
EDUCATION KIDS
www.BabyProfessorBooks.com
to download Free Baby Professor eBooks
and view our catalog of new and exciting
Children's Books